HOW TO PRAY IN ISLAM FOR GIRLS

SCAN QR CODE
WITH YOUR
PHONE TO VIEW
ALL OUR BOOKS

PUBLISHED BY

TABLE OF CONTENTS

INTRODUCTION

Let's Learn How to Talk to Allah!

Assalamu Alaikum, little friends!

Welcome to our special book where we're going to discover something **amazing** together—how to talk to Allah!

Do you know what that's called?

It's called "Salah"!

Imagine having a *secret code* to talk to the kindest, most loving friend in the whole universe.

That friend is Allah, and Salah is our special way of connecting with Him.

What is Salah, you ask?

Salah is a **special time** when we stand, bow, and kneel to talk to Allah.

It's like having a friendly chat with the One who made the stars twinkle and the flowers bloom.

And guess what?

We get to do this **five** times a day!

Can you believe it?

That's because Allah **loves** hearing from us regularly, just like our parents love hearing about our day.

Why Should We Learn?

Learning how to pray Salah helps us feel closer to Allah, like we're sharing our secrets and dreams with Him.

Plus, it's a little like planting *seeds of goodness* in our hearts every time we pray.

Our Prophet Muhammad
(peace and blessings be upon him) said,

"On the Day of Judgment, a slave will be questioned about his prayers first. If his prayers are good, his other deeds will be good, too. If his prayers are bad, his other deeds will be bad, too."

(Tabarani, Targhib)

CHAPTER 1: UNDERSTANDING SALAH

Why is Salah so, so special?

Imagine you have a *treasure* chest, and inside it, there's happiness, peace, and love.

Salah is like opening that treasure chest and filling our hearts with all those wonderful feelings.

When we pray regularly, it's like adding more and more *jewels* to our treasure chest.

So, Salah is not just a talk; it's like a wonderful *journey* that makes our hearts sparkle with joy!

How the Salah Helps Us

1. Spiritual Superpowers:

Salah connects us to Allah, making our hearts *strong* and full of **kindness**. It's like turning on a spiritual light inside us that guides us to do good things and make the right choices.

2. Mental Energy:

Have you ever felt a bit confused or worried? Well, Salah is like a super **calming** potion for our minds. It helps us focus better and fills our heads with positive thoughts!

3. Healthy Hearts and Bodies:

When we move and stretch during Salah, it's like giving our bodies a little exercise. Our muscles become strong, and our bodies feel **energized**—like little superheroes ready to take on the world!

Prayer Checklist

Facing the Qiblah 

When we pray, we face a special direction—towards the Kaaba in Mecca. It's like pointing our hearts directly to where Allah's house is. Cool, right?

Intention (Niyyah)

Before we start Salah, we think in our hearts, "I'm going to talk to Allah now." So, before we begin, we have this special feeling inside, a promise to connect with Allah.

The Role of Concentration

Concentration helps us really, really focus on talking to Allah. Imagine you're coloring in your favorite coloring book, and you want to stay inside the lines. Concentration in Salah is a bit like that.

CHAPTER 2: THE WUDU (ABLUTION)

Wudu is Like a Mini Water Party

Imagine you're playing in the water on a hot
summer day.

Wudu is a bit like that, but even better!

It's our special way of cleaning up before we stand
in front of Allah.

So, get your imaginary water buckets ready
because we're about to have a Wudu party!

Why is Wudu So Special?

Wudu is more than just water and splashing fun.

It's about getting our **hearts, mind and body** ready to talk to Allah.

When we do Wudu, it's like putting on a special superhero **costume** that makes us feel extra close to Allah.

It's a way of saying, "I'm getting ready for the most **important** conversation ever!"

Our Prophet Muhammad
(peace and blessings be upon him) said,

"When a Muslim performs ablution, his sins are removed from his hearing, his sight, his hands, and his legs."

(Musnad Aḥmad)

The Order of Wudu

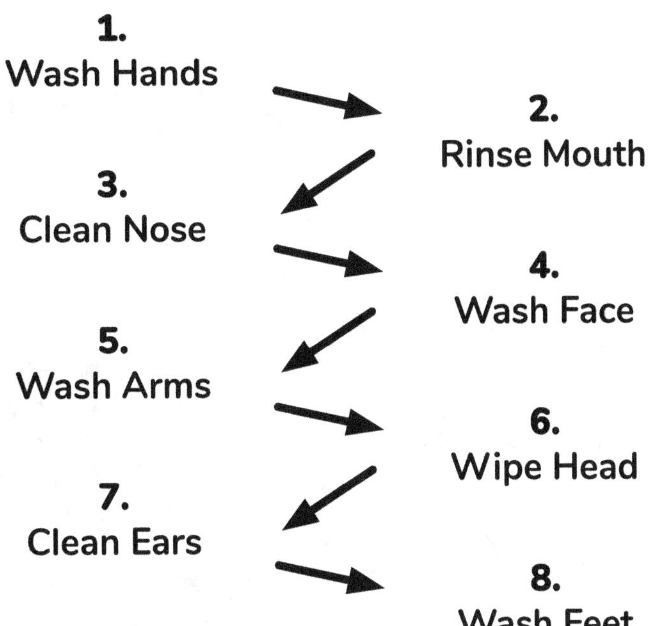

1. Wash Hands

Start by saying Bismillah and then wash your hands three times, beginning with the right hand and extending to the wrist and between the fingers.

2. Rinse Mouth

Using your right hand, take a handful of water and rinse your mouth three times.

❸ Clean Nose

Using your right hand, take a handful of water, sniff it into your nostrils, and let out three times.

❹ Wash Face

Wash your face three times, stretching from the chin to the hairline and from ear to ear.

5. Wash Arms

Wash your arms three times up to the elbows, beginning on the right.

6. Wipe Head

Wipe your head starting at the front, moving all the way to the back, then returning to the front.

7. Clean Ears

Use your forefingers to clean the inside grooves of your ears and your thumb to clean the back.

8. Wash Feet

Wash your feet three times, beginning with the right foot, up to your ankles and in between your toes.

Dua After Wudu

Our beloved Prophet Muhammad (peace be upon him)
said that if we say the following dua after wudu, then
so many of our small bad deeds get washed away!

Arabic Text:

أَشْهَدُ أَنْ لا إِلَهَ إِلاَّ اللهُ

وَحْدَهُ لا شَرِيكَ لَهُ

وَأَشْهَدُ أَنَّ مُحَمّداً

عَبْدُهُ وَرَسُولُه

Transliteration (Saying the Words in English):

'Ash-hadu 'an laa 'ilaaha 'illallaahu
wahdahu laa shareeka lahu
wa 'ash-hadu 'anna Muhammadan
'abduhu wa Rasooluhu.

English Translation (What the Words Mean):

I bear witness that none has the right
to be worshipped except Allah,
alone without partner,
and I bear witness that Muhammad
is His slave and Messenger.

Tayammum

Did you know that if you don't have access to water
you can still pray Salah by doing Tayammum.

Allah says in the Quran, chapter 4 verse 43;
"If you cannot find any water, then do tayammum with
pure earth"

How to do Tayammum:

1. Find a section of land clear of dirty elements

2. Say Bismillah

3. Put your hands on the earth surface

4. Clear excess dust off your hands

5. Rub your hands together

6. Gently wipe both hands over your face

CHAPTER 3: THE ADHAN (CALL TO PRAYER)

What's That Beautiful Sound?

The adhan is a call to prayer, a bit like a friendly **invitation** to join a beautiful conversation with the One who loves us the most.

The Adhan is not just any melody; it's like a golden key that unlocks the doors to a **special time** with Allah.

When we hear the Adhan, it's like Allah saying, "Hey, my dear friends, come and talk to Me. I'm here, and I'm listening."

Learning the Words

Arabic Text:

اَللَّهُ اَكْبَرُ - اَللَّهُ اَكْبَرُ

اَللَّهُ اَكْبَرُ - اَللَّهُ اَكْبَرُ

اَشْهَدُ اَنْ لَا اِلَاهَ اِلَّا اللهُ

اَشْهَدُ اَنْ لَا اِلَاهَ اِلَّا اللهُ

اَشْهَدُ اَنَّ مُحَمَّدًا رَسُولُ اللهِ

اَشْهَدُ اَنَّ مُحَمَّدًا رَسُولُ اللهِ

حَيَّ عَلَى الصَّلَاةِ - حَيَّ عَلَى الصَّلَاةِ

حَيَّ عَلَى الْفَلَاحِ - حَيَّ عَلَى الْفَلَاحِ

اَللَّهُ اَكْبَرُ - اَللَّهُ اَكْبَرُ

لَا اِلَاهَ اِلَّا اللهُ

Transliteration (Saying the Words in English):

Allahu Akbar, Allahu Akbar

Allahu Akbar, Allahu Akbar

Ashhadu an la ilaha illallah

Ashhadu an la ilaha illallah

Ashhadu anna Muhammadan rasulullah

Ashhadu anna Muhammadan rasulullah

Hayya 'ala as-salah, Hayya 'ala as-salah

Hayya 'ala al-falah, Hayya 'ala al-falah

Allahu Akbar, Allahu Akbar

La ilaha illallah

English Translation (What the Words Mean):

Allah is the Greatest, Allah is the Greatest

Allah is the Greatest, Allah is the Greatest

I bear witness that there is no god but Allah

I bear witness that there is no god but Allah

I bear witness that Muhammad is the Messenger of Allah

I bear witness that Muhammad is the Messenger of Allah

Come to prayer, Come to prayer

Come to success, Come to success

Allah is the Greatest, Allah is the Greatest

There is no god but Allah

CHAPTER 4: THE FIVE DAILY SALAHS

Fajr
(The Morning Adventure)

Two Rak'at Sunnah | Two Rak'at Fard

Imagine waking up when the world is still asleep, and the sky is like a big, soft blanket filled with stars.

Fajr is our first **private talk** with Allah.

It's like having a cozy, quiet conversation with Allah to start our day.

We stand tall, bow down, and kneel, whispering our secrets to the One who created the sun and the moon.

Dhuhr

(The Midday Break)

Four Rak'at Sunnah | Four Rak'at Fard | Two Rak'at Sunnah

When the sun is right above us, it's time for Dhuhr!

This chat is like a **sunshine break** in the middle of our day.

We stand, bow, and kneel, saying, "Hey, Allah, thanks for the yummy lunch and the fun we had today."

Asr

(The Afternoon Pause)

Four Rak'at Fard

Afternoon is playtime, but before we dive into our toys, it's time for Asr!

Asr is like a **special pause button** in our day, where we connect with Allah before jumping back into our daily adventures.

Maghrib

(The Evening Rest)

Three Rak'at Fard | Two Rak'at Sunnah

As the sun starts to set, it's Maghrib time!

We pray, saying, "Thank you, Allah, for the fun, the laughter, and **good times** today."

Isha

(The Nighttime Talk)

Four Rak'at Fard | Two Rak'at Sunnah

When the sky is like a big, dark canvas filled with twinkling stars, it's time for Isha!

We share our nighttime **dreams and wishes** with Allah.

Isha is our way of saying, "Goodnight, Allah, thanks for being our best friend all day."

Salah Timings

Fajr - This is the first prayer, performed at dawn and ending when the first light appears, or the start of twilight.

Dhuhr - This is the second prayer, and it is said at Asr time, starting when the sun starts to set.

Asr - When an object is the same size as its shadow, the third prayer takes place. Asr ends when the sun starts to fade just before dusk.

Maghrib - This is the fourth prayer, and it should be offered as soon as possible, even though it is still valid until Isha. It begins when the sun sets.

Isha - This is the fifth prayer, and it is said at the exact moment when the twilight's red hue fades. It must be completed in the first half of the night.

Fajr

Dhuhr

Asr

Maghrib

Isha

CHAPTER 5: HOW TO PRAY SALAH

Dress Code and Etiquette

Imagine you're getting ready for a royal tea party, but this time, it's with Allah! Here's how you can dress like a super-princess for Salah:

1. Cover Your Hair with a Beautiful Hijab:

Just like wearing a sparkly crown, a hijab is a *beautiful* way to cover your hair during Salah.

2. Wear a Long, Flowy Dress:

For Salah, wear something long and flowy that covers your arms and legs. From your neck to your toes, imagine wrapping yourself in a cozy royal robe. It's like creating a beautiful and modest look fit for a princess during Salah.

Lastly, if you *brush your teeth* using a siwak before you begin praying then you can increase the rewards you receive from the Salah.

Praying Two Raka'at

We will now show you how to perform a a Salah with two units of prayer (raka'at) to help you understand the different movements in Salah.

Face the direction of the Kabaa and then focus on your intention to pray to Allah.

Then begin the prayer with Takbir.

1. Takbir

Raise your hands towards your shoulders and say:

اللَّهُ أَكْبَرُ

Allahu Akbar

(Allah is the Greatest)

2. Standing and Reciting

After saying takbir, place your hands over your chest with your right hand over the left.

Point your eyes to the place where your forehead will touch the floor, then say the following:

أَعُوذُ بِاللَّهِ مِنَ الشَّيْطَانِ الرَّجِيمِ

Authubillahi minashaytaan-nirajeem

(I seek refuge in Allah from the cursed Satan)

Then we say:

بِسْمِ ٱللَّهِ ٱلرَّحْمَـٰنِ ٱلرَّحِيمِ

Bismillaahir Rahmaanir Raheem

(In the Name of Allah—the Most Compassionate, Most Merciful)

Then recite Surah Al-Fatiha followed by another Surah. You can find the Surahs in Chapter 7, Page 57.

☡ Ruku (Bowing)

Say the following as you bow:

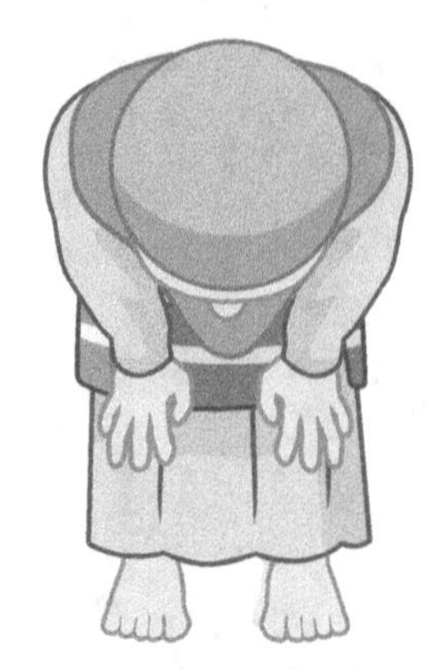

اللَّهُ أَكْبَرُ

Allahu Akbar

(Allah is the Greatest)

As you bow your head down, place your hands on your knees and keep your back as straight as you can.

When you are in the bowing position, quietly say (three times):

سبُحانَ ربِّي العظيمِ

Subhaana rabbiyal 'adheem

(How perfect is my Lord, the Magnificent)

4. Back to Standing

Return to standing and say:

سَمِعَ اللَّهُ لِمَنْ حَمِدَهُ

Sami Allahuliman hamida

(Allah hears those who praise Him)

Then quietly say:

ربَّنا ولك الحمدُ

Rabbana walakal hamd

(Our Lord, to You is all praise)

5. Sujud (Prostration)

As you are moving to the sujud position say:

اللَّهُ أَكْبَرُ

Allahu Akbar

(Allah is the Greatest)

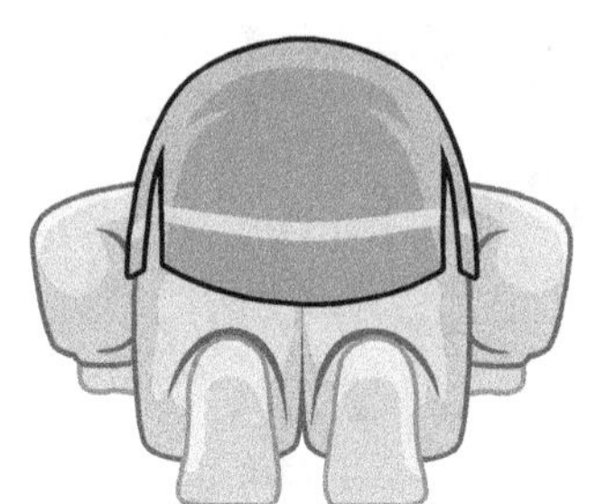

Make sure your elbows are kept off the floor and that your nose, forehead, knees, both palms, and toes are all in contact with the ground.

When you are in this position say quietly (three times):

سُبْحَانَ رَبِّيَ الْأَعْلَى

Subhaana rabbiyal a'laa

(How perfect is my Lord, the Most High)

6. Sitting Position

As you sit up from sujud say:

اللَّهُ أَكْبَرُ

Allahu Akbar

(Allah is the Greatest)

In the sitting position quietly say (twice):

رَّبِّ اغفر لِي

Rabbigh-fir lee

(O my Lord, forgive me)

7. Back to Sujud (Prostration)

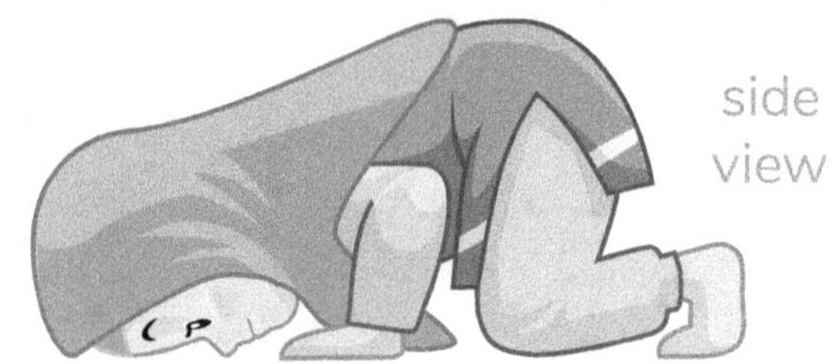

As you are returning back to the sujud position say:

اللَّهُ أَكْبَرُ

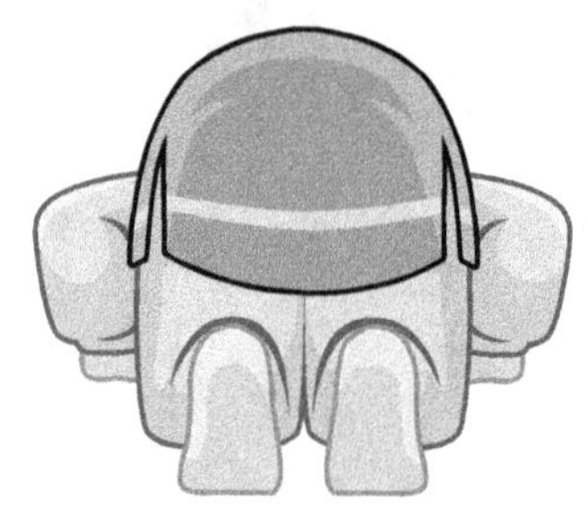

Allahu Akbar

(Allah is the Greatest)

When in sujud again say quietly (three times):

سُبْحَانَ رَبِّيَ الْأَعْلَى

Subhaana rabbiyal a'laa

(How perfect is my Lord, the Most High)

৪ Back to Standing

Rise from sujud back to the
standing position, ready for the
next unit of prayer, and say:

اللَّهُ أَكْبَرُ

Allahu Akbar

(Allah is the Greatest)

Perform the second rak'ah (unit) of prayer by
repeating the previous steps 2 to 7.

The Tashahhud (sitting position)

After the second rakaah, we reach the Tashahhud.

When in the Tashahhud sitting position, raise your right index finger, and quietly recite the first part of the Tashahhud on the next page.

The first part of the Tashahhud is recited after the second rak'ah of Dhuhr, Asr, Maghrib and Isha.

The final part of the Tashahhud is recited in the second rak'ah of Fajr, the third rak'ah of Maghrib and the fourth rak'ah of Dhuhr, Asr and Isha.

'Abdullah ibn 'Umar said: "When the Prophet (peace and blessings be upon him) sat during the prayer, he would place his right hand on his right thigh and clench all his fingers, and point with the finger that is next to the thumb, and he would place his left hand on his left thigh." (Sahih Muslim)

front
view

side
view

rear
view

The First Part of Tashahhud

Arabic Text:

التَّحِيَّاتُ لِلَّهِ وَالصَّلَوَاتُ وَالطَّيِّبَاتُ

السَّلَامُ عَلَيْكَ أَيُّهَا النَّبِيُّ وَرَحْمَةُ اللَّهِ وَبَرَكَاتُهُ

السَّلَامُ عَلَيْنَا وَعَلَى عِبَادِ اللَّهِ الصَّالِحِينَ

أَشْهَدُ أَنْ لَا إِلَهَ إِلَّا اللَّهُ وَحْدَهُ لَا شَرِيكَ لَهُ

وَأَشْهَدُ أَنَّ مُحَمَّدًا عَبْدُهُ وَرَسُولُهُ

Transliteration (Saying the Words in English):

At-tahiyyatu lillahi was-salawatu wat-tayyibatu

As-salaamu 'alaika ayyuhan-nabiyyu wa rahmatullahi wa baraktuhu

As-salaamu 'alaina wa 'ala 'ibaadillahis-saaliheen

Ash-hadu an laa illaha illallahu wa ash-hadu anna muhammadan

'abduhu wa rasuluhu

English Translation (What the Words Mean):

All the compliments are for Allah and all the prayers and all
the good things
Peace be on you, O Prophet, and Allah's mercy and blessings
And peace be on us and on the good worshipers of Allah
I testify that none has the right to be worshipped but Allah
and that Muhammad is His slave and Messenger

The Final Part of Tashahhud

Arabic Text:

اللَّهُمَّ صَلِّ عَلَى مُحَمَّدٍ وَعَلَى آلِ مُحَمَّدٍ

كَمَا صَلَّيْتَ عَلَى إِبْرَاهِيمَ وَعَلَى آلِ

إِبْرَاهِيمَ إِنَّكَ حَمِيدٌ مَجِيدٌ

اللَّهُمَّ بَارِكْ عَلَى مُحَمَّدٍ وَعَلَى آلِ مُحَمَّدٍ

كَمَا بَارَكْتَ عَلَى إِبْرَاهِيمَ وَعَلَى آلِ

إِبْرَاهِيمَ إِنَّكَ حَمِيدٌ مَجِيدٌ

Transliteration (Saying the Words in English):

Allahumma salli 'ala Muhammad wa 'ala aali Muhammad

Kamaa sallayta 'ala Ibraaheem wa 'ala aali Ibraaheem innaka

hameedun majeed

Allahumma baarik 'ala Muhammad wa 'ala aali Muhammad

Kamaa baarakta 'ala Ibraaheem wa 'ala aali Ibraaheem innaka

hameedun majeed

English Translation (What the Words Mean):

O Allah! Praise Muhammad, and on the followers of Muhammad
As You Praised Ibraaheem, and the followers of Ibraaheem; You
are indeed Worthy of Praise, Full of Glory
And send blessings on Muhammad, and on the followers of
Muhammad
As you sent blessings on Ibraaheem, and the followers of
Ibraaheem; You are indeed Worthy of Praise, Full of Glory

Tasleem

After completing the Tashahhud, we end the Salah by doing the Tasleem.

Do the first Tasleem by looking to the right and saying:

السَّلَامُ عَلَيْكُمْ وَرَحْمَةُ اللهِ وَبَرَكَاتُهُ

Assalaamu alaykum wa rahmatullah

(May peace and the mercy of God be upon you)

Do the second Tasleem by looking to the left and saying:

السَّلَامُ عَلَيْكُمْ وَرَحْمَةُ اللهِ وَبَرَكَاتُهُ

Assalaamu alaykum wa rahmatullah

(May peace and the mercy of God be upon you)

Now, the Salah is completed!

CHAPTER 6: ADHKAR AFTER SALAH

Our Prophet Muhammad
(peace and blessings be upon him) said:

"The angels invoke blessings on any of you who
remains in his prayer place as long as he does not
invalidate his ablution, saying, 'O Allah, forgive him; O
Allah, have mercy on him.'"

[Maalik, Al-Bukhari and others]

ADHKAR ONE

Immediately after Salah, say the following:

أَسْتَغْفِرُ اللَّهَ، أَسْتَغْفِرُ اللَّهَ، أَسْتَغْفِرُ اللَّهَ

Astaghfirullaah, Astaghfirullaah, Astaghfirullaah

(I seek the forgiveness of Allah)

Then say:

اللَّهُمَّ أَنْتَ السَّلَامُ، وَمِنْكَ السَّلَامُ،
تَبَارَكْتَ يَا ذَا الْجَلَالِ وَالإِكْرَا

Allaahumma 'Antas-Salaamu wa minkas-salaamu,
tabaarakta yaa Thal-Jalaali wal-'Ikraam

(O Allah You are the Flawless One, and from
You comes peace and security. Blessed are You,
Possessor of Majesty and Honour)

ADHKAR TWO

Say the following three words thirty-three times each:

سُبْحَانَ ٱللَّهِ	Subhanallah	(Allah is free from imperfections)
ٱلْحَمْدُ لِلَّهِ	Alhamdulillah	(All praise is for Allah)
ٱللَّهُ أَكْبَرُ	Allahu Akbar	(Allah is Greater than anything)

Then end with the following:

لا إلَهَ إلاّ اللّٰهُ وَحْـدَهُ لا شريكَ لهُ، لهُ الملكُ ولهُ الحَمْدُ، وهُوَ على كُلّ شَيءٍ قَـدير

Laa 'ilaaha 'illallaahu wahdahu laa shareeka lahu, lahul-mulku wa lahul-hamdu wa Huwa a'laa kulli shay'in Qadeer

(There is no god but Allah, the One, having no partner with Him. Sovereignty belongs to Him and all the praise is due to Him, and He is Potent over everything)

ADHKAR THREE

Our Prophet Muhammad
(peace and blessings be upon him) said,

"Whoever recites the verse of the Throne (Ayatul Kursi)
after every obligatory prayer, there will be nothing standing
between him and his entering Paradise except death."

(An-Nasa'i)

اللَّهُ لاَ إِلَهَ إِلاَّ هُوَ الْحَيُّ الْقَيُّومُ لاَ تَأْخُذُهُ سِنَةٌ

وَلاَ نَوْمٌ لَهُ مَا فِي السَّمَاوَاتِ وَمَا فِي الأَرْضِ

مَنْ ذَا الَّذِي يَشْفَعُ عِنْدَهُ إِلاَّ بِإِذْنِهِ يَعْلَمُ مَا

بَيْنَ أَيْدِيهِمْ وَمَا خَلْفَهُمْ وَلاَ يُحِيطُونَ بِشَيْءٍ

مِنْ عِلْمِهِ إِلاَّ بِمَا شَاءَ وَسِعَ كُرْسِيُّهُ السَّمَاوَاتِ

وَالأَرْضَ وَلاَ يَئُودُهُ حِفْظُهُمَا وَهُوَ الْعَلِيُّ الْعَظِيمُ

Allahu la ilaha illa Huwa, Al-Haiyul-Qaiyum La ta'khudhuhu sinatun wa la nawm, lahu ma fis-samawati wa ma fil-'ard Man dhal-ladhi yashfa'u 'indahu illa bi-idhnihi Ya'lamu ma baina aidihim wa ma khalfahum, wa la yuhituna bi shai'im-min 'ilmihi illa bima sha'a Wasi'a kursiyuhus-samawati wal ard, wa la ya'uduhu hifdhuhuma Wa Huwal 'Aliyul-Adheem

(Allah! There is no god (worthy of worship) except Him, the Ever-Living, All-Sustaining. Neither drowsiness nor sleep overtakes Him. To Him belongs whatever is in the heavens and whatever is on the earth. Who could possibly intercede with Him without His permission? He (fully) knows what is ahead of them and what is behind them, but no one can grasp any of His knowledge—except what He wills (to reveal). His Seat encompasses the heavens and the earth, and the preservation of both does not tire Him. For He is the Most High, the Greatest.)

CHAPTER 7: SURAHS TO LEARN

The first surah we will learn is called Surah Al-Fatiha,
which is the opening chapter of the Quran. This surah
is recited in every rak'ah of every Salah.

After this, we will learn four of the shortest surahs
that can be found in the Quran to make it easy for you
to learn and memorise them.

Seeking Allah's Protection (Al-Isti'aadha)

Before we begin to recite a surah from the Quran,
we must recite the following:

أَعُوذُ بِٱللَّهِ مِنَ الشَّـيْطَٰنِ ٱلرَّجِيْمِ

A'udhu billahi minashaytaanir-rajeem

(I seek refuge in God from the accursed devil)

SURAH AL-FATIHA

Chapter 1 in the Quran

Arabic Text:

ٱلْحَمْدُ لِلَّهِ رَبِّ ٱلْعَٰلَمِينَ

ٱلرَّحْمَٰنِ ٱلرَّحِيمِ

مَٰلِكِ يَوْمِ ٱلدِّينِ

إِيَّاكَ نَعْبُدُ وَإِيَّاكَ نَسْتَعِينُ

ٱهْدِنَا ٱلصِّرَٰطَ ٱلْمُسْتَقِيمَ

صِرَٰطَ ٱلَّذِينَ أَنْعَمْتَ عَلَيْهِمْ

غَيْرِ ٱلْمَغْضُوبِ عَلَيْهِمْ وَلَا ٱلضَّآلِّينَ

Transliteration (Saying the Words in English):

Alhamdu lillaahi Rabbil 'aalameen

Ar-Rahmaanir-Raheem

Maaliki Yawmid-Deen

Iyaa kana' budu wa iyaa kanasta-'een

Ihdinas-Siraatal-Mustaqeem

Siraatal-latheena an'amta 'alayhim

ghayril-maghdoobi 'alayhim wa lad-daaalleen

English Translation (What the Words Mean):

All praise is for Allah—Lord of all worlds,

the Most Compassionate, Most Merciful,

Master of the Day of Judgment,

You [alone] we worship and You [alone] we ask for help.

All praise is for Allah—Lord of all worlds,

the Path of those You have blessed

not those You are displeased with,

or those who are astray

SURAH AL-KAWTHAR

Chapter 108 in the Quran

إِنَّآ أَعْطَيْنَـٰكَ ٱلْكَوْثَرَ

فَصَلِّ لِرَبِّكَ وَٱنْحَرْ

إِنَّ شَانِئَكَ هُوَ ٱلْأَبْتَرُ

Innaaa a'taynaa kal kawtharr

Fasalli li-rabbika wan harr

Inna shaani-aka huwal ab-tarr

Indeed, We have granted you [O Prophet] abundant goodness

So pray and sacrifice to your Lord [alone]

Only the one who hates you is truly cut off [from any goodness]

SURAH IKHLAAS

قُلْ هُوَ ٱللَّهُ أَحَدٌ

ٱللَّهُ ٱلصَّمَدُ

لَمْ يَلِدْ وَلَمْ يُولَدْ

وَلَمْ يَكُن لَّهُ كُفُوًا أَحَدٌ

Qul huwallahu ahad

Allahussamad

Lam yalid walam yoolad

Walam yakullahu kufuwan ahad

Say, [O Prophet,] "He is Allah—One [and Indivisible];

Allah—the Sustainer [needed by all]

He has never had offspring, nor was He born

And there is none comparable to Him

SURAH AL-FALAQ

Chapter 113 in the Quran

قُلْ أَعُوذُ بِرَبِّ ٱلْفَلَقِ

مِن شَرِّ مَا خَلَقَ

وَمِن شَرِّ غَاسِقٍ إِذَا وَقَبَ

وَمِن شَرِّ ٱلنَّفَّٰثَٰتِ فِى ٱلْعُقَدِ

وَمِن شَرِّ حَاسِدٍ إِذَا حَسَدَ

Qul a'oothu bi rabbil-falaq

Min sharri maa khalaq

Wa min sharri ghaasiqin ithaa waqab

Wa min sharrin-naffaa-thaati fil 'uqad

Wa min sharri haasidin ithaa hasad

Say, [O Prophet,] "I seek refuge in the Lord of humankind

From the evil of whatever He has created,

And from the evil of the night when it grows dark,

And from the evil of those (witches casting spells by) blowing

onto knots,

And from the evil of an envier when they envy."

SURAH AN-NAS

Chapter 114 in the Quran

قُلْ أَعُوذُ بِرَبِّ ٱلنَّاسِ

مَلِكِ ٱلنَّاسِ

إِلَـٰهِ ٱلنَّاسِ

مِن شَرِّ ٱلْوَسْوَاسِ ٱلْخَنَّاسِ

ٱلَّذِى يُوَسْوِسُ فِى صُدُورِ ٱلنَّاسِ

مِنَ ٱلْجِنَّةِ وَٱلنَّاسِ

Qul a'oothu bi rabbin-naas

Malikin-naas

Ilaahin-naas

Min sharril waswaasil khannaas

Allathee yu was wisu fee sudoorin-naas

Minal jinnati wannaas

Say, [O Prophet,] "I seek refuge in the Lord of humankind

The Master of humankind

The God of humankind

From the evil of the lurking whisperer

Who whispers into the hearts of humankind

From among jinn and humankind."

CHAPTER 8: TIPS FOR PARENTS

Start with Super Simplicity

Begin with the basics! Teach one move at a time and *celebrate* each small victory.

It's like learning the ABCs before reading a whole story.

Simple Demonstrations

Parents and educators, become superhero role models! Show the moves of Salah with *enthusiasm*.

It's *contagious*, and soon, little superheroes will want to join the adventure.

Use Reward Charts

Create a fun *reward chart*, and every time they achieve something, add a sticker.

The more stickers, the more happy they feel!

Patience and Encouragement

Be their super *cheerleader*!

Patience is your blessing, and encouragement is your superpower.

Kids are like seeds—water them with praise, and watch them grow!

Celebrate Small Achievements

Every small move learned is a *victory!*

Celebrate with high-fives, hugs, or a little treat.

Create a Special Salah Corner

Make a *cozy* Salah corner!

Add soft pillows, twinkling lights, and maybe a favorite teddy or toys.

CHAPTER 9: ANSWERING COMMON QUESTIONS

Q: Why do we pray five times a day?

A: Praying five times a day is like having five special moments to connect with Allah. It's our way of saying, "Allah, you're always in our hearts, no matter what we're doing!"

Q: What if I forget a part of Salah?

A: No worries, little superhero! If you forget a part, you can add it at the end or say sorry to Allah and try again next time. Allah knows we're learning, and He loves our efforts.

Q: Why do we face the Kaaba in Makkah during Salah?

A: Facing the Kaaba is like facing the special direction Allah asked us to. It's a bit like turning our hearts toward His house, showing that no matter where we are, we're all connected.

Q: Can I talk to Allah about anything during Salah?

A: Absolutely! Allah is like our best friend who loves to hear everything on our minds. You can talk to Him about your happy moments, your worries, and even ask for His help.

Q: Can I pray Salah in my own words?

A: While we have special words for Salah in Arabic, you can also speak from your heart. Imagine you're telling Allah about your day in your own words. He loves to hear your beautiful voice.

Q: Why do we make certain movements during Salah?

A: Each move has a special meaning. It helps us focus and show respect to Allah. The movements also keep our bodies healthy and strong.

CHAPTER 10: GLOSSARY OF KEY TERMS

Allah:

Allah is the Arabic word for God—the One who created everything, including superheroes like us!

Salah:

Salah is our superhero chat with Allah. It's a special time when we stand, bow, and kneel to talk to Him.

Qiblah:

Qiblah is the special direction we face during Salah, towards the Kaaba in Mecca. It's like pointing our superhero hearts to the superhero home.

Niyyah:

Niyyah is the superhero intention we have before Salah. It's like saying, "Hey, Allah, I'm here to chat with You!"

Adhan:

Adhan is the musical call to prayer, like a superhero melody inviting us to talk to Allah.

Wudu:

Wudu is the magical water party we have before Salah. It's like splashing our hands, faces, and feet to get ready for the superhero adventure.

Ruku:

Ruku is the superhero bowing move in Salah. It's like saying, "Allah, you're the greatest!"

Sujud:

Sujud is the superhero kneeling move in Salah. It's like giving Allah a big, warm hug with our hearts.

Tashahhud:

Tashahhud is the superhero sitting break in Salah. It's like saying, "Phew, that was an awesome chat, Allah!"

Adkhar:

Adhkar is to remember Allah after Salah or any time during the day and say certain words that our Prophet Muhammad (peace and blessings be upon him) taught us to say. These words give us so much peace, and Allah also rewards us with good deeds when we say these Adhkar.

Kaaba:

The Kaaba is a special building in Mecca. Facing the Kaaba during Salah is like pointing our superhero compass in the right direction.

Rakʿah (plural: raka'at):

It is a single prayer unit that fits inside the movements needed to offer Salah.

Fard:

These are the prayers that we must pray five times a day as Muslims.

Sunnah:

An extra Salah that can be offered in addition to the five daily Salahs is known as a Sunnah prayer. The 12 raka'at of the Sunnah prayers are divided into the following five daily prayers: two before fajr, four before dhuhr and two after dhuhr, two after maghrib and two after isha.